iMath
Readers

# The Mystery Beetle:
## What's Multiplying?

**by John Perritano**

Content Consultant
David T. Hughes
*Mathematics Curriculum Specialist*

NORWOOD HOUSE PRESS
Chicago, IL

Norwood House Press
PO Box 316598
Chicago, IL 60631

For information regarding Norwood House Press, please visit our website at
www.norwoodhousepress.com or call 866-565-2900.

Special thanks to: Heidi Doyle
Production Management: Six Red Marbles
Editors: Linda Bullock and Kendra Muntz
Printed in Heshan City, Guangdong, China. 208N—012013

**Library of Congress Cataloging-in-Publication Data**

Perritano, John.

The mystery beetle: what's multiplying?/by John Perritano; content consultant
David Hughes, mathematics curriculum specialist.
pages cm.—(iMath)

Audience: 8-10
Audience: K to grade 3

Summary: "The mathematical concept of multiplication is introduced as
readers learn about all different types of beetles and how many beetles are
in a museum. Different multiplication methods include modeling, repeated
addition, skip counting, using an array, and creating a multiplication
expression. Includes a discover activity, an art and history connection, and
mathematical vocabulary introduction"—Provided by publisher.

Includes bibliographical references and index.

ISBN 978-1-59953-557-9 (library edition : alk. paper)
ISBN 978-1-60357-526-3 (ebook)

1. Multiplication—Juvenile literature. I. Bullock, Linda. II. Title.

QA115.P4665 2013
513.2'13—dc23
2012023838

# CONTENTS

**Note to Caregivers:**

Throughout this book, many questions are posed to the reader. Some are open-ended and ask what the reader thinks. Discuss these questions with your child and guide him or her in thinking through the possible answers and outcomes. There are also questions posed which have a specific answer. Encourage your child to read through the text to determine the correct answer. Most importantly, encourage answers grounded in reality while also allowing imaginations to soar. Information to help support you as you share the book with your child is provided in the back in the **Additional Notes** section.

**Bold** words are defined in the glossary in the back of the book.

## What's That in Your Hand?

It is black and white. It has six legs and two pairs of wings. The wings in the front are hard. They fold neatly over the wings in the back. Its outer skeleton is made of tough plates.

What is this animal that you hold in your hand? It is a mystery to you.

## Museum Mystery

You think about the different ways you can identify the strange insect in your hand. Suddenly, you remember there is a museum nearby. It has a huge insect collection.

At the museum, you go to the Insect Room, where you can search for a beetle like the one in your hand. There are 10 cabinets along each of four walls. Each cabinet is filled with drawers. The beetle could be in any one of them.

How many cabinets are in the room? How can you find out?

**Idea 1:** You could make a **model** to find the answer. You could draw and count the cabinets. Or, you could use objects to make the model.

Do you think using a model is a good way to find how many cabinets there are? Why or why not?

**Idea 2:** You could use a **number line** to help you find the total through **repeated addition**. Repeated addition means to add by the same number. For example, 10 + 10 + 10 + 10.

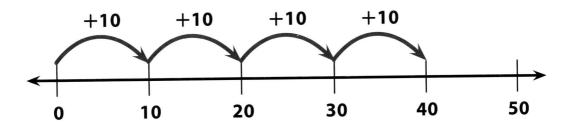

Do you think using a number line is a good way to find how many cabinets there are? Why or why not?

**Idea 3:** You could **skip count** to find out how many cabinets there are in all.

There are 10 cabinets along each wall. And, there are 4 walls. So, skip count by 10 four times.

10, 20, 30, 40

You could also use a **hundred chart** to help you skip count accurately.

### Hundred Chart

| 1 | 2 | 3 | 4 | 5 | 6 | 7 | 8 | 9 | 10 |
|----|----|----|----|----|----|----|----|----|-----|
| 11 | 12 | 13 | 14 | 15 | 16 | 17 | 18 | 19 | 20 |
| 21 | 22 | 23 | 24 | 25 | 26 | 27 | 28 | 29 | 30 |
| 31 | 32 | 33 | 34 | 35 | 36 | 37 | 38 | 39 | 40 |
| 41 | 42 | 43 | 44 | 45 | 46 | 47 | 48 | 49 | 50 |
| 51 | 52 | 53 | 54 | 55 | 56 | 57 | 58 | 59 | 60 |
| 61 | 62 | 63 | 64 | 65 | 66 | 67 | 68 | 69 | 70 |
| 71 | 72 | 73 | 74 | 75 | 76 | 77 | 78 | 79 | 80 |
| 81 | 82 | 83 | 84 | 85 | 86 | 87 | 88 | 89 | 90 |
| 91 | 92 | 93 | 94 | 95 | 96 | 97 | 98 | 99 | 100 |

Do you think skip counting is a good way to find how many cabinets there are? Why or why not?

**Idea 4:** You could make an **array.** An array has an equal number of objects in each row.

Draw ten symbols in one row. Draw four rows in all.

10 groups of 4 is the same as 10 × 4.

The total is the **product.**

Do you think making an array is a good way to find the answer? Why or why not?

**Idea 5:** Write a **multiplication problem** and solve.

10 × 4 = ?

$$\begin{array}{r} 10 \\ \times\ 4 \\ \hline ? \end{array}$$

Do you think writing and solving a problem is a good way to find how many cabinets there are? Why or why not?

**Materials**
- a set of objects, such as paper clips or pebbles used in a fish tank
- paper and pencil

## Grouping Objects

Look around the room. Find lots of one thing that you can use to try different ways to count. Paper would work. So would the pebbles used in fish tanks.

Or, go outside to collect objects such as pebbles or fallen leaves.

Spill the objects onto a table. Organize them into groups. What do you notice about the groups? What could you do to make them easy to count?

Now, let's say that you want to know how many objects you have in all. There are many ways you can find out. Which way will you use?

- a model
- a number line
- skip counting
- an array
- a multiplication problem that you solve

Choose a way you like best to find the total number of objects you have.

Then, challenge yourself to use a different way to check your answer. The product should be the same. But what happens if you get two different answers? What will you do?

 **What's the Word?**

Look for *The Beetle Book* by Steve Jenkins. Read more about beetles that stink, bite, glow, squirt poisons, and dash from danger.

You choose a drawer. It is filled with colorful beetles. They are often in your garden at home. These are ladybird beetles.

Most beetles have two pairs of wings. The two wings in the front are hard and thick. They cover and protect the second pair of wings.

A ladybird beetle's bright colors warn other animals that it tastes bad.

Ladybird beetles are small and usually yellow, orange, or bright red. Their bodies are often covered with small black spots. Do you know why they are colorful?

Ladybird beetles release a liquid from their legs. The bright colors say, "I taste awful! Stay away!"

Look at the picture below. It shows the ladybird beetles in an array inside the drawer. Each row has an equal number of beetles.

How many ladybird beetles are there in all?

**Did You Know?**

About 40% of all insects are beetles.

## Cowboy Beetles

You open another drawer. Inside is a collection of cowboy beetles. They are golden brown with a black stripe down the middle.

Cowboy beetles fly among flowers on summer days. They are large beetles and make a loud noise when they fly. Their noise and their color help keep them safe. Do you know why?

Some adult cowboy beetles like this one spend their entire lives living in a single garden.

The cowboy beetle sounds and looks like a wasp! That keeps many **predators** away.

There are 4 rows of cowboy beetles in the drawer. There are 9 beetles in each row. How many cowboy beetles are there in all?

9 beetles in each row
4 rows of beetles

Use repeated addition and a number line to find the answer.

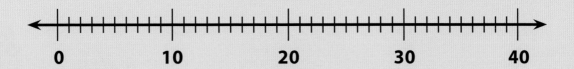

Click beetles like this one can snap
body parts to jump away from danger
and to frighten away enemies.

## Click Beetles

Snapping beetles. Spring beetles. They are both click
beetles. Guess how they got their names.

Sometimes, a beetle falls on its back. It's hard
for most beetles to get up again. But it's easy for
click beetles.

A click beetle snaps two parts of its upper body
together. The snap sounds like a click. The beetle pops
up into the air. Then, it lands on its feet.

You open a new drawer. Inside are 4 rows of click beetles. There are 15 beetles in each row.

How many beetles are there in all? Skip count to find the answer. Use a hundred chart to help you skip count accurately.

**Hundred Chart**

| 1 | 2 | 3 | 4 | 5 | 6 | 7 | 8 | 9 | 10 |
|---|---|---|---|---|---|---|---|---|---|
| 11 | 12 | 13 | 14 | 15 | 16 | 17 | 18 | 19 | 20 |
| 21 | 22 | 23 | 24 | 25 | 26 | 27 | 28 | 29 | 30 |
| 31 | 32 | 33 | 34 | 35 | 36 | 37 | 38 | 39 | 40 |
| 41 | 42 | 43 | 44 | 45 | 46 | 47 | 48 | 49 | 50 |
| 51 | 52 | 53 | 54 | 55 | 56 | 57 | 58 | 59 | 60 |
| 61 | 62 | 63 | 64 | 65 | 66 | 67 | 68 | 69 | 70 |
| 71 | 72 | 73 | 74 | 75 | 76 | 77 | 78 | 79 | 80 |
| 81 | 82 | 83 | 84 | 85 | 86 | 87 | 88 | 89 | 90 |
| 91 | 92 | 93 | 94 | 95 | 96 | 97 | 98 | 99 | 100 |

## Fireflies

Click beetles can give off light. So can fireflies.
Fireflies are a different kind of beetle.

Some male fireflies flash light to attract females. When
a female sees the flashes, she answers with light.

You open a new drawer. Inside are 11 rows of fireflies.
Each row has 9 fireflies. How many fireflies are there
in all? Write a multiplication problem and solve.

$$11 \times 9 = ?$$

$$\begin{array}{r} 11 \\ \times\ 9 \\ \hline ? \end{array}$$

## Dung Beetles

Some dung beetles roll balls of dung, or animal waste. Others live in it or burrow through it.

Dung is filled with food. Adult dung beetles drink the liquid inside the dung. Young beetle **larvae** (LAR-vee) eat the dung.

You open a drawer filled with 7 rows of dung beetles. You count 10 beetles in each row. How many dung beetles are there in all? How will you find out?

## Rhino Beetles

What's large, powerful, and has horns on its head? It's a male rhino beetle! There are more than 300 kinds of rhino beetles. They include the Hercules beetle, unicorn beetle, ox beetle, and elephant beetle.

The names tell you that these beetles are really strong. A rhino beetle can lift something 850 times heavier than itself. What is the greatest weight you have ever lifted?

You count 12 groups of 3 beetles in a drawer. How many beetles are there in all?

## Stag Beetles

A stag is a male deer. Almost all stags have antlers. They use their antlers to battle other stags.

Stag beetles also use their antlers for battle. The antlers aren't true antlers. They are the male's huge lower jaw.

Female stag beetles have long jaws, too. But they are shorter than the male's. She can use her jaws to bite. Ouch!

How did the stag beetle get its name?

You count 3 rows of male stag beetles and 3 rows of female stag beetles. There are 9 beetles in every row. How many stag beetles are in the drawer?

There are more than 700 kinds of water beetles on Earth, one of which is the whirligig beetle.

## Whirligig Beetles

A spinning toy is called a whirligig. Water beetles are also called whirligigs. They swim in circles if they sense danger. They swim round and round.

Whirligig beetles have two sets of eyes. One pair is on top. The other is on bottom. So, the beetle can see both above and under the water at the same time.

You open a drawer and find 10 rows of 10 whirligigs. How many beetles are there in all?

# Jewel Beetles

Artists once used jewel beetle wings to make jewelry and decorations. Some still do.

A beetle's colors depend on how you look at it. Its outer covering reflects light. Change the angle you look at the beetle. Then, you'll see different rainbow colors of light.

There are more than 15,000 species of jewel beetles in the world.

One drawer has 12 rows of jewel beetles. Each row holds 5 beetles. How many jewel beetles are there in all?

# Connecting to History

Soon after beetles mate, they die. Long ago in Asia, workers picked up millions of dead beetle bodies each year. Then, they shipped them to India. Indian artists sewed the beetle wings onto cloth.

In the 1800s, some English women wore living beetles. They used tiny gold chains to hold them to their clothes. Many of the beetle wings sewn onto cloth remain shiny even after the cloth has rotted.

 **Did You Know?**

Even today, artists use jewel beetles to make art. In 2002, artist Jan Fabre used about 1.6 million beetle wings to decorate the ceiling of the Royal Palace of Brussels in Belgium.

# Math at Work

**Entomologists** study insects. Say an entomologist wants to know how many ants live in a hole. She marks each ant she sees with a tiny spot of paint. She counts as she marks the ants.

Then, she comes back another day. She counts ants with marks and ants without marks. She adds to find how many ants there are in all.

Then, she multiplies.

Total Number of Ants on Day 1
× Total Number of Ants on Day 2
‾‾‾‾‾‾‾‾‾‾‾‾‾‾‾‾‾‾‾‾‾‾‾‾‾‾‾‾‾‾‾

Next, she divides the product by how many marked ants she counted on Day 2.

The **quotient** is close to the number of ants that live in the hole.

Some entomologists do their work outdoors, or in the field.

# The Mystery Is Solved

You open a drawer. There are only two beetles inside, and they look exactly like yours! There is also a rolled-up poster inside. You unroll it carefully.

The beetle in your hand and those in the drawer are serious pests. They are Asian longhorned beetles. People around the country are working to stop the pest from spreading.

The Asian longhorned beetle is originally from China.

Female beetles lay eggs in hardwood trees. Grubs hatch from the eggs. Then, they turn into larvae. The larvae chew their way into the heart of the tree. They live there all winter.

The life cycle is almost complete. Each larva wraps itself in a **cocoon** (kuh-KOON). Inside the cocoon, the larva changes into an adult.

Adult beetles leave the tree in spring to find mates. By this time, the tree is dead.

If 5 females each lay 20 eggs in a total of 5 trees, how many eggs will they lay in all? How many trees will die?

How will you find out?

**Idea 1:** Building **models** works well. But you will need to draw or find lots of objects to solve this problem.

**Idea 2:** You can use a **number line** to do **repeated addition**. But you will have to decide how to divide and label your line. This could take some time.

**Idea 3:** You can **skip count,** but it may be hard to use mental math in this problem.

**Idea 4:** You can draw an array. But that will take time and paper and pencil.

**Idea 5:** You can write and solve a **multiplication problem**. This will probably be the fastest way to find how many eggs the female beetles laid.

How many eggs did the beetles lay in all? How many trees will die?

Great job! You identified the mystery insect and used multiplication to accomplish your mission! Now it's time to go home and see if you can find Asian longhorned beetles in your trees!

# WHAT COMES NEXT?

Imagine how many trees would die if there were more than five female beetles in the woods.

In some states, students search for signs that a female has laid eggs. They report what they observe, and the trees are burned. This kills the pests before they become adults and mate.

The holes show where beetles have made tunnels in the tree. The tree will probably need to be cut down.

How could you check to be sure that no Asian longhorned beetles live near you? You may want to form a volunteer group. Together, you could learn how to find signs that females are nearby. Your work could save trees, in your neighborhood and in forests far from where you live. You could become an eco-hero.

# GLOSSARY

**array:** things organized in equal rows and equal columns. For example, you can arrange 12 jelly beans into an array of 3 rows of 4 jelly beans.

**cocoon:** a case some insects make to stay safe during the change from larva to adult.

**entomologists:** scientists who study insects.

**hundred chart:** a chart with 10 rows and 10 columns showing numbers 1 through 100.

**larvae (LAR-vee):** the young forms that hatch from many insect eggs. Larvae grow in size. In time, each larva forms a pupa. Inside the pupa, the larva changes into its adult form.

**model:** objects or pictures that you use to show a process or solve a problem.

**multiplication problem:** a set of numbers and symbols that represent a relationship, such as $3 \times 5 = 15$.

**number line:** a diagram that uses points on a line to represent numbers.

**predators:** living things that hunt other living things for food.

**product:** the result you get when you multiply.

**quotient:** the result you get when you divide.

**repeated addition:** repeating the same addend over and over again. Multiplication is a shortcut for repeated addition.

**skip count:** to find a product by counting equal groups of two or more objects.

# FURTHER READING

FICTION
*James and the Giant Peach,* by Roald Dahl, Penguin Classics, 2011
NONFICTION
*The Beetle Book,* by Steve Jenkins, Houghton Mifflin Books for Children, 2012
*Insect Detective,* by Steve Voake, Candlewick Press, 2010
*What Can We Do about Invasive Species?,* by Lorijo Metz, PowerKids
    Press, 2010

# ADDITIONAL NOTES

**The page references below provide answers to questions asked throughout the book. Questions whose answers will vary are not addressed.**

**Page 6:** There are 40 cabinets; $4 \times 10 = 40$

**Page 10:** Making equal groups would make them easier to count.

**Page 11:** Help children understand why it is important to try different multiplication strategies to find correct answers.

**Page 13:** There are 30 ladybird beetles.

**Page 15:** There are 36 cowboy beetles.

**Page 17:** There are 60 click beetles.

**Page 18:** There are 99 fireflies.

**Page 19:** There are 70 dung beetles.

**Page 20:** There are 36 rhino beetles.

**Page 21:** There are 54 stag beetles. Caption question: Children may guess that because the male beetle's lower jaws are described as antlers, these beetles make people think of deer. One name for a male deer is a stag.

**Page 22:** There are 100 whirligig beetles.

**Page 23:** There are 60 jewel beetles.

**Pages 27–28:** $20 \times 5 = 100$ eggs in all. 5 trees will die.

# INDEX

# CONTENT CONSULTANT

**David T. Hughes**

David is an experienced mathematics teacher, writer, presenter, and adviser. He serves as a consultant for the Partnership for Assessment of Readiness for College and Careers. David has also worked as the Senior Program Coordinator for the Charles A. Dana Center at The University of Texas at Austin and was an editor and contributor for the *Mathematics Standards in the Classroom* series.